REMARKS

"*I've had a look at your website, and talented. Such gorgeous, evocative imagery. I have no doubt you'll find the right home for your beautiful work soon.*"

All my best,

Jack

Jack Jewers: Managing Director

www.moonflowerbooks.co.uk

"*Our curators just read your story, Soaring, that you submitted for review. Based on its quality, they selected it to be recommended to readers interested in Poetry across our homepage, app, topic page, and emails. Thanks for writing.*"

Your friends at Medium

Austin Publishers

editors@austinmacauley.com

"*My colleagues and I have been discussing various aspects of your collection and have agreed that your poems are well-written with an eclectic range of themes throughout, we see potential in the work.*"

James Houghton
Commissioning Editor
Olympia Publishers

Erica B. Donaldson-Ellison

Searching For An Oasis

Erica B. Donaldson-Ellison

If you purchased this book without a cover, you should be aware that this book is stolen property. It was reported as "unsold and destroyed" to the publisher, and neither the author nor the publisher has received any payments for this "stripped book."

Searching For An Oasis

Copyright © 2021 by Erica B. Donaldson-Ellison

Cover Design by N. D. "Indy" Brennan
Cover Photo by Erica B. Donaldson-Ellison

Website: www.just-saying.blog

No part of this publication may be reproduced, stored in a retrieval system, or transmitted in any form or by any means, electronic, mechanical, photocopying, recording, or otherwise, without the written permission of the publisher. the only exception is brief quotations in printed reviews. For information regarding permission, contact the authors at edonaldsonellison@gmail.com.

This book was originally published by arrangement with MADDCity Media.

Erica B. Donaldson-Ellison, Authors

Searching For An Oasis/Erica B. Donaldson-Ellison – First Edition

1. Poetry 2. Social 3. Racism

4. Black History 5. Black Women 6. Equality I. Donaldson-Ellison, Erica B., author II. Title

ISBN- 9798491190157

Published by arrangement with Erica B. Donaldson-Ellison and N. D. "Indy" Brennan.

All rights reserved.

First Edition.

Typeset Arial

DEDICATIONS

For Mama, Papa, and Stephen who taught me all I know.

Erica B. Donaldson-Ellison

THEME ONE
LOVE
1. Butterfly kisses
2. Soaring
3. Celebrate Health
4. Early Morning Mist
5. Comfort
6 Parting
7. By Myself

THEME TWO
WORK
8. Rage
9. Stand up and be Counted
10. Colour Blindness
11. Unfulfilled
12. Distaste
13. Growth
14. Noise
15. Gettin'up that hill

THEME THREE
FAMILY
16. Quiet Man
17. Colour
18. Stolen loves
19. A Simple Exchange
20. Poor - Part One and Part Two
21. Clarity
22. Oasis

THEME FOUR
SPIRIT
23. So, It is written
24. Freedom
25. Groundhog Day
26. It's Always 3am
27. Affirmation
28. Pride
29. Sunshine
30. Beginning

THEME FIVE
TRAVEL IN TIME AND SPACE
31. Hope
32. The wind changes
33. Heart Food
34. Ypres
35. Fine Dining
36. Microaggressions
37. Childhood Hurt
38. New Way to Walk
39. A Slight Breeze
40. Meditation
41. Cleansing Waters
42. An Inner Light
43. Wanting
44. Lightning
45. Overwhelmed
46. Trees of Life
47. Alive, Autumn
48. A New Day
49. Streets of Napoli
50. Lift my Soul
51. The Apple Tree

SEARCHING FOR AN OASIS

Theme One

LOVE

Erica B. Donaldson-Ellison

Poem Number 1

Butterfly Kisses
30/3/2016

Lovin' you
deep kisses for the hurt
Butterfly caresses for each scene
Red wine flushes away anger
lost moments, in-between.

Water quenches wrinkles
Colour for the grey
Masking hours, running on
Ease the pain, away

Fleeting, lunging, thoughtlessness
Emotive grasps
Objects broken
Family treasures lost.
Haunting moments
Searching eyes
Unspoken insults.

How to mask the troubled hurts?
Detailed anguish, uniquely measured
ruined seconds
which, could have been spent
in, other pursuits of pleasure

procreating memories
detailing kindnesses
Deep kisses
Would have, never been required
to erode, a pain, that was
never meant to be inflicted

Butterfly apologies
Wing away
the hurt.

Poem Number 2

Soaring
21/09/2020

Let me soar with you
blackbird
Let us fly
far, far from here
leave my worries behind
speckled tombs below me
On earth

Poem Number 3

Celebrate Health
2/4/2016

You are beautiful to watch
Amazing
Bright, alert eyes
stretching, arms
Torso, relaxed
Connections, synapses
closing
Jutting arse
Flexed arms
All serviced
With, a smile
how did you
come to be?

Raphaelite curls
a family trait
caresses a bent head
concentrated on the task.
Limbs lengthen
to reach, their goal
in a crouching, slow extension
relaxing in a rhythmic motion
and, I can only imagine
the unclothed version
basking in the sun
Aaaaaahhhh!
Just messin........

Poem number 4

Early Morning Mist
17/2/2017

Piercing peals of birdsong, herald daybreak
Cutting sheets of misty dew
I am captured, as I watch
dipping beaks taste raindrop puddles
Startled, staccato, spider legs, are wet
As they peck at sparkling pools

Leaves unfurl and catch
early sunshine rays
And, condensation begins to quench
the thirst of, crackled, crispy grass

A bountiful scene emerges
An unveiling

Nature hums praise
to the living earth

A beauty extends
stretching past
horizons. Dimming
way beyond our sight
and, a mist surrounding us parts
As I stare
And gaze
with you

Poem Number 5

Comfort
27/6/2019

Is this where
        you want
                to be?
Suffused in softness

is this where
        you want
                To be?
Warm
Content
    Loved

Poem Number 6

Parting
1/2/2019

I am planning how to leave you
Learning how to say 'goodbye'
Staring, mentally etching
Making memories of your face
Looking at your fingertips
Painting pictures
Remembering, every line
Marking the expressions which
feed, your soul
Searching for an essence
Learning , how to
Feel…you
So that
I can smile, a goodbye
and not
Breakdown
And cry.

Poem Number 7

By Myself
27/12/2018

I am cold
Hollow bone
Empty to the core

Trembling goosebumps
Expanding circles of
Blown, balloon, bubbles
of, emptiness

Aching shudders
Icy length of
Muscular atrophy
Shorten

How can I be warm, when
you are not nearby
within an arm's reach
to hold?

Theme Two

WORK

Erica B. Donaldson-Ellison

Poem Number 8

Rage
26/7/2017

Though

Once again

Unfounded

Brittle accusations

Crackle, on the air.

And, a mirrored fixation

Stares

Directly

At them.

They do not see

Oppression

Reverberating Rage

Glancing back

At them.

Yet

Standing tall

We, shall not

Splinter.

We, cannot

Break.

Rather, we shall

Stand

Lift our heads

Laugh

And smile

Conquer

An, institutionalised racism

Rise above it.

And

Succeed

Though

You may

Doubt it.

We will

Consistently

Without tears

Implement an historic

Systematic strategy

And, we will

Endure.

A cocoon gestation

Into

Brilliant butterfly

Alive

In a triumphant, celebration

Of, our own education

And, of our own

Unique talents.

They

Cannot control

Our spirits

We will

Not

Break.

Poem Number 9

Stand Up and Be Counted
5/3/2017

Just because

You say that:

'It has to be

Like that.'

Approved, without conscience

Driven by: uneducated criticism

And stereotypic non-consensual nonsense.

A single dissenter

Can still rise

SEARCHING FOR AN OASIS

Blooming, from the crowd

And, say

NO

The chatter of group compliance

Simmers gently, without a spill

But, a lone ingredient

May yet spark a quicker bubble.

It unexpectedly spurts

Volcanic lava

Overflowing

Making a small trail.

Like the person, who

Demonstratively argues

Their cause.

Stands and brings attention

And, says

NO.

Moved by the need

To right, a wrong

Disgust, peaked by

Witnessed exchanges

Of a bullies attempt to dominate

A 'weaker person'.

I say

NO.

To team sly glances

Highlighting an

Underlying group aversion

To an individual's

Differences.

I say

NO.

Upright. Tall.

Against, sneering grins

Smeared across

Grinning lips.

Authoritatively, I protest

And say

NO.

Then,

Walk on.

With my own

Smile.

Leading the way.

Poem Number 10

Colour Blindness
3/7/2019

Why?

Should we

Search for colour

When it just

Happens?

A creation, that is

Something

Uniquely beautiful

All around us.

It was never

Meant to be

Thrust

In front of us

As a yardstick measure

Of superiority.

Precious moments happen

Because of

The content of

Someone's character

And, personality

And not because of

Their skin colour.

Poem Number 11

Unfulfilled
28/6/2017

I, cannot sleep
because
I am
ashamed
of what
I do

I cannot rest
I seek
a blessing
A, reassurance of who
I am?

Sweet
enticing delights
Delicate, desserts
Sugar coated, enticements
flute glasses of bubbling cava
encourage me, to- forget

As I devour
satiating sweetmeats
distracting treasures
I fulfil
an
Empty, need

Poem Number 12

Distaste
24/10/2018

How is it with me, that
a kind word from a stranger
can cause me to falter
Reduce me to tears

How is it with you, that
Although, I have
the right to be respected
that is so difficult for you
to do

Poem Number 13

Growth
4/1/2019

If, an unkind word
from a stranger
a comment from someone
commences you to self-punish
causes you to feel fear

Remember to

Reflect

Breathe

Centre yourself

Stretch the hurt out

Find yourself

Seek out your friends

Self-doubt

Seeks safety

In self-love

Yearns only

For kindness

Flip the image

That their unkind words or treatment

May have begun:

You
Are
Enough

Poem Number 14

Noise
8/8/2020

If it was for the purposes of
exchanging information
or for the praising of actions
perhaps an acknowledgement of interactions
or for the sharing of love
then, I should smile

But, the chatter and the shouts
Voices raised without communicating
Just for the sake of the sound
As if as a declaration of an existence
Like the qualification of dominance over another
person's voice
a crass intrusion to a party
to which they were not invited
raising their own voice
just for
the sake of it
encompasses the entirety of the description
that evokes all
that, I can
hear

Poem Number 15

Gettin' Up That Hill
18/3/2019

If when I look at my path
The road seems steep
An end, touching a level
which claims a cloudless sky

Beyond my reach
a higher peak
a climb that
makes me weary
just to look

And, as I stare
heaving a sigh
lost, lonely
ready to forget it
giving up before
even commencing it
contemplating an endless unattainable goal

Yet, a memory of
my Grand mama's smile appears
before me
and my heart begins to sing
starting with a tentative glow
which flickers gently
slowly at first
kindling a dampened fire

Smouldering embers
gain momentum

as I remember
A glorious warmth erupts
ignited from my memories of my Mama's
determined stances

When faced with hypocrisy
or someone telling her 'No'
she simply continued
steadfast
smiling with that contagious inner glow
which used to burn gloriously
in my younger years
when Mama commanded
urging me to: lift my head up high

"Look ahead
Just begin
Take
one step
Just take
one step
at, a time"

Theme Three

FAMILY

Erica B. Donaldson-Ellison

Poem Number 16

Quiet man

2/1/2019

Standing guard

A

Quiet

    Man
who   marks the time
with a cigarette

Watching over
standing guard

Making safe
watching us

Whilst we played

Standing guard
protecting us
        as we grew

A quiet man
Standing
Smiling
    Guarding us

pushing,   developing his children's skills.
urging us to live
 Tell me
     who

Looked after you?

Poem Number 17

Colour
31/3/2016

Red, for anger
Soothed by beckoning blue
Towards heavenly heights
Blinding streaks of yellow sunlight
Invoke ,a
Thought of mystical blue
Black and white skins
Delightfully merge
Into a triumphant cream
Stand tall, little one
You are rooted
In fertile soil
Reach towards the sky
burst
A rainbow

Poem Number 18

Stolen Loves
27/8/2020

Throw your tears
Across our path
we will cry
those tears
That you
Cannot shed

Poem Number 19

A Simple Exchange
13/7/2020

Whenever I would chance to meet

Another blackface

More often than not

Our eyes would smile at one another

and, we would exchange

a simple acknowledgment

of the other person's existence,

a nod

A shared understanding,

a greeting

Sometimes, a knowing wink

Sometimes a raised eyebrow-sufficed

Because in that

Simple acceptance

The message was communicated

"I know you....stranger

I understand what has been happening in your life"

We share the same type of encounters

We both know of the treatment that has come to us

We are both aware of

What the other has endured, during their day

We have both been met

With similar practices and behaviours

By colleagues as well as strangers

Both received sceptical glances

SEARCHING FOR AN OASIS

When introduced to people who don't

know us

We are used to 'that look'

From a person who obviously does not

trust us

Because they harbour an ignorant

prejudice

Before they get to know us, as individuals

We both have been surprised

When small children of our

acquaintances

Ask out loud "why is your skin darker"

Than most people that they know in their own circle

We both hope that

Their parents will learn to teach their children

About

Diversity and culture

We both despair that

We are looked at

And treated differently

When in a crowd

We are used to being singled out

Discriminated

When we are doing our best at just

Trying to fit in

We may not be able

To know each other's skills

Nor say each other's names

We may not know

Each other's specific age

But, we do share

The same hope's for our futures

So, when I exchange a greeting

With a stranger in the street

And, my friends and my young children

Often say "You know a lot of people"

I reply:

"I do not know them personally but

I do know how they live."

Poem Number 20

Poor (In Two Parts)
4/3/2017

Part One

Is there poverty, in a young girl

And her sisters

Who, together

Carry the family wash

Laundered at the local Laundromat

Mamas' brood of children

Plus mum and Dad

Who chauffeur all

On a family trip, to the seaside

Black and white photos show

Smiling faces

Posing, munching fish and chips

Four bags- shared

Each, had a meal, made up

Equal to their appetite.

See: Look at the

Satisfied, grinning faces.

We always had

                Enough

SEARCHING FOR AN OASIS

Were we ignorant?
Not understanding that
We were
Underprivileged?
We were certainly not
Undernourished!

I remember:
Overflowing plentiful bowls of
Slices of ripe juicy watermelon
That we had
When we played out
On a hot day
Behind the back of our
Terraced home.
We, Washed the sweet red fruit
down, with
tumblers of carrot juice
which was, freshly grated
by Mama and Papa
Then, hand squeezed into
shards of ice
Diluted with frothy, creamy milk
Topped with Guinness
We were-

Happy Children!

There were

Stimulating and exciting

Post office parcels

Delivered to our house.

Heavy on the mat.

Saturday educational

                         grammar workbooks

which we dutifully filled

(some of us, quicker than others)

grouped around the dining table

Schooled and tutored by, Papa

Who taught each one of us at

Our own level.

Adjective verbs, naming nouns and

Those annoyingly complex, mathematical equations.

We all sat

In our dining places, where

earlier, we had had

bowls of steaming porridge

And then huge plates of

beans and bacon

We ate until our stomachs were

SEARCHING FOR AN OASIS

Heavily laden.

Each year, at Christmas
always, a sock
for each child
Filled with a new watch
or a Special gift, for the older ones
Plus: Tangerines, oranges and chocolates.
All secured by the means of weekly payments
at the local shop
Routinely done, by Mama.
Should we have been saddened
Did our lack of knowledge
make us
      Ignorant?

Part Two

I remember
Evenings, surrounded by
Snow encrusted windows
We were warmed by
Coal fires;
The shared, family red rug
Where we huddled
Listening to
the radio,
Or, in the front room
one of us
practised playing the piano
And, the rest of us
all , argued, in one room
about, whose turn it was, to
choose,
the TV programme on
The black and white channel.

Once a week
we each ate
A melted Cadbury
Chocolate chunk

Or a flavour from

The Neapolitan, ice cream block.

It was bought, to

celebrate

the arrival of

The brown paper, wage packet

that Papa handed to Mama

And that she

rhythmically, separated

in order to pay each

household bill; whilst the eldest child present,
was given and took possession of the treat

And was responsible to ensure that

It was

    "Equally divided

Amongst "us.

One chocolate square each: Another half or two
- If we were lucky

It could be made to last, a

Whole evening!

It tasted and melted like

"Our own whole bar of chocolate!"

Should we each have

been critical

Thrown a tantrum, because

we did not all have

A whole one?

Monday to Friday, we
happily, went to school -
Looked forward to it
Wore one clean, pressed uniform daily
One in the wash
One ready to put on
Did we need more?
Were we really
           Poor?

At home
we changed into play clothes
Had seriously competitive
Marble competitions.
Using colourful, fashionable bags
which we had carefully sewn together
Cobbled with
Our own shaky needlepoint.
Sometimes
we organised
Running races.
I remember
It was agonizingly painful

waiting to be picked
As a good team player.

You know, when I
Look back
on my childhood
I am content that
it was a
      Happy one.

When I was younger
Life was:
      Simpler.
I had not yet learnt
how to want or
How to be
ungrateful

Poem Number 21

Clarity
29/7/2020

Is it slippery out?
I went in with two of me
Exited as one personality
Unencumbered by dual thoughts

Poem Number 22

Oasis
3/4/2016

There is a place
where my family meet
A haven where
Time has no meaning
and, the clock on the wall
remains permanently still
at two minutes past five.
Since, the pressures of work
Simply melt
At the door.

An oasis of calm
Captured in
A pleasant surrounding
where, we can reflect
On our feelings
Without fear
Of condescension

It is, where
We all can
Rest
And
Relax

We are safe
In the comforting arms
Of people
Who we love

And who do
Love us, back.

Relationships are explored
Clarified and
Allowed to ferment
Cherished and permitted
Within, a safe environment

Anything goes
where, everyone
Is loved
For themselves
Love has
No boundaries
All is
Allowable

Heartfelt remembering's
Can surface
And, there *is* time
Free from technology
To enjoy, watching
Butterflies, in the sun
And, our frayed nerves
Are afforded
The opportunity
To heal
Where we are
Unencumbered by
The excesses of competition
A reprieve
From the madness
Of a life
In the work situation

It is a haven
Where, we can
Be
Real and true
To ourselves

Our oasis
Allows us
To demonstrate
Freedom of expression
In it,
We are free to
'Ramble on'
We are safe
Protected, from
Criticism or judgement
Cascading from the world
We learn to
Forgive
Ourselves
As well as
To forgive, others

Physical neglect
Is not permitted
Nourishment is important
Prioritised, so that
With satisfied stomachs
Our minds and spirits
Can escape
And rest

Everyone is loved
Without judgment
Free from stereotypes

We do not tolerate
Intruders
For, our own manners
Are known
And -reasonably accepted
By-each other
So
The welcome
Is
Warmer
For
Family and close friends, only
Everyone, present
Is loved
For themselves

It is a protected place
Where, we
Purge our cares
And our worries
Cherish our thoughts
Replenish
Our souls
Mull on our memories
And our concerns
Our senses excite and soar
We care
For, each other
We prioritize our lives

It is our refuge
Of calm
A place
Where, we
Can begin
To rejoin

Our minds
And, our hearts
Within a heavenly haven
That we call
"Our Home"

Theme 4
SPIRIT

Poem Number 23

So, it is written
31/3/2016

So
It is written
And, therefore shall come to pass
Life is pre-planned
Or is it just
A winding path?
The scent of senses
Oozes from my skin
And, you are the 'light'
You are my air
You are my breeze

I am
Many people's
I hear you call
While snow cascades
While autumn leaves fall
I laugh with you
As the bluebells spring
And the wind rushes
And while new life is born

Did I dream it
When you said
'Come walk with me?"
When I awake
You
Are gone-disappeared
Was it only
A dream?

Poem Number 24

Freedom
30/3/2016

I heard it said that
'We are free!'
Free to live
Free to achieve
And so, we live
Knowing that
What 'they did'
In dying for us
And I chase
This one life
Remembering them

Proud with direction
Light and focused
On pure ascension
Choosing, to love
Embracing one truth
So, blatantly clear

Yet, a single domination
May deflect the drive
For a goal
Embittered wounds
Punish our souls

And, we falter
Deflected from the task
Falling from steps
That seemed, steadfast

But, we were meant
To carry 'one dream'
Founded in lost centuries
Carried in streams of
Blood generations
Powered by toil
Strong in its movement
Contained in earth's, very soil

Future generations
Carry our plight
Live out our dreams
Embrace our desires

For, **YOU are Free!**
Relight our fires
Cherish our pasts
Life is - Yours

You are free
To love
When, you can choose to love
Why, inflict hurt?
Love, your life
Empower
Now
Live
Live life
For your ancestors!

Poem Number 25

Groundhog Day
31/4/2016

There was something
I must do
Something
I need to grasp….
It was
So warming
When I was asleep
But, dismissed
When I awoke
I can
No longer
Feel, it
So
In searching for
Lost senses
Routine is found

Quick
Seize the day
Eat, work
Less time, for play
Than I would have liked

I may recall
When
Relaxed in bed
As I close my eyes, that
That which eluded my day
Was……
I forgot

To make, the time
To love
Again!

Poem Number 26

It's Always Three AM
2/4/2016

Sleep escapes
At 3am
Night-time's feasts
Give no release
To guilt
The body
Will not
Relax
Whilst the soul
Battles with
Searches for
Solving paths, to
Should've, would've
Could've grief

We awake
To empathetic tears
Sacrificed for those
Who we sense
Are sad

We must
Breathe….

Seeking purging thoughts
It helps
If we
Let the light in

SEARCHING FOR AN OASIS

Each sunrise, is
A birth
Of new situations
Today
Matters
There will
Never be
Another one
The same
Seize each second

A moment is
Was and always
Will be
Treasured
Hours of experience
Can be
Celebrated
Witnessed by
The elegance in
Honest hairs of grey

Use, your best self
To retaliate, revitalise
Interact
Armed with
This basic knowledge
Use, your
Inner
Power

Poem Number 27

Affirmation

I
Am
Me
I am growing my own voice
I will
Become
My own team

Poem Number 28

Pride
11/7/2017

I do not exist
Inside a box
Of your choosing
You-cannot
Contain me
No man's arms
Can encircle me
Though
You do still, love me
Eloquently put
I, cannot be squashed
To fit
Into
A size
That, I am not
I am
Vast
No mould
Can contain me
I have a smile that
Encompasses all
That, I am
A laughter that spreads
Stating who
You think that
I am
Creates no fact
Interrupting me
Disrupting, my expression
Does not erase

The content of
My sentence
I challenge
Sneering looks of
Hostility
Pride
Is not
Penetrable
It is not negotiable
And cannot be controlled
Nor directed
By arrogant hostility
Like breath
But, not needing
Oxygen to live
It just
Is
Always haunting
Whether you
Want it to
Or not
Possessed by a passion
Pride, forever
Fights back

Poem Number 29

Sunshine
15/2/2017

Through, closed eyes
I can see
a radiant surge
a bright pulsing sun
and, my heart
Beats on

Toes, tickle
Pebbled grains of stone and sand
Awaken, sensitive nerves
Stimulates glands
and, my heart
Beats on

Sunshine warms my skin
Tingling gooseflesh dances
Reflexively reaching out a thanks
And, my heart
Beats on

Amid wisps of otherwise
Still skies
A floating gust
A lighter breeze
Caresses my lips
Conducts them into
A curling smile

As I feel
I sense warmth
A rising praise, inside
And, my heart beats on

As I catch
The very last of
The dipping warm rays
Which stream
Forcing a tear to erupt
Squeezed, through stinging eyes
And, my heart beats on
To, a slower
Rhythmic lullaby

Poem Number 30

Beginning
12/10/2020

Sunshine, streaking
Through the blinds
Each new day brings
A new venture
To be
Embraced

Erica B. Donaldson-Ellison

Theme Five

TRAVEL IN TIME AND SPACE

Erica B. Donaldson-Ellison

Poem Number 31

Hope
1/4/2016

Mama's curse
The action, or
A person
Who may
Cause her children
To cry

Tearful emotions
Thus expressed
Are preferable
To   despairs
Otherwise felt
Alone
Hidden in silence

a pure   empathetic tear

marks a concern

It signifies that
Another person   IS

Alive.

And open

To anothers

Human misery

There is

A future

For mankind

In such a feeling

Promise
lights the hope in

Our   children's
       smiles

Poem 32

The Wind Changes
1/4/2016

When we arrived
A winter's chill
Pervaded

Twigs and, autumn leaves cascaded
At   our front door
a cold
     Silence

Nature   hibernated
Lonely dogs
        howled.

Yet
children   played
throughout, as young
one's do,
Cajoling nature's
turnaround. And
the small one's
we can see, are
overshadowed by
brother's, sister's
friends, who are
leggier
More assertive
in loco parentis
as they teach
new tasks
Albeit   newly learned.

In the distance
I can see
lambs and kids
Offspring of goats.

Additional bells   chorus the
change   of the season
new life erupts
With hopes
Of
rebirth

Sprigs on the vines
Carry, a promise
of a good wine
this year

like the caterpillars
That storm our home
we know that
We   will   emerge
from moth
to   Butterfly
Spring   has
Come!

March, disappears
with   a   vengeance

April, Angels
wing   us   on
towards   home

Fruit blossoms   bloom
and, we   will

generate a
blessed
           fruit

Poem 33

Heart food
23/4/2016

Time, to nourish the body
Quench   an inner thirst
cherish, building blocks of love
Heart food
for
our
souls

Turn, towards the living
remembering looks of   reflection

Smiling, winsome glances
love a spirit
towards   it's heaven

laugh, the moments
onward
ease,a memory
outward

Soon enough
we   all   will   be
just, a passing memory

Time, to live
our, own   lives

happy   to   be
just, within
only,   the   living

of it

I
Am
MANY, peoples
God   IS: good

It IS   TIME to
move   on

It is TIME to
go   forward

to those who have passed
we call......
"We soon
        Come"

Poem number 34

Ypres
28/5/2016

Lively, sunburnt poppies flutter
Visitors
momentarily, stare
whilst crowds
collect, in fields of sorrow
Black birds
swarm
amongst intricate spirals
Upward thrusts
extend, towards
The spires in Ypres
A city
suffused with culture
where
I loved, the
Blinding, beating sun
when it
Penetrated
the crusty, crackled
Greying paintwork
Rays reflected
rippled ochre greys
sandstone browns   of
stone.
The beating, battling
blues of Ypres
why did this place, not
love me, back?

Our souls are buried

SEARCHING FOR AN OASIS

beneath your pavements

Butchered

Limbs, left

headless, helmets

No longer
protecting our
    brains

brightly coloured cyclists
panniers bounce   gaily, where
battles once raged
fertile fields of our blood
Interned with
fountains   of   tears
from
our weeping mums
and our daughters

Life
Stumbles along
whilst
we   sleep
Enmasse

our families
Fix on
Lost   heroes
lost   moments
Fleeting loves
escaped   feelings
never fully lived

still

a hummingbird   flutters
against, humps of greenbacks
caravans now
pass   us

our families   measure moments
Grieving for
lost   grandfathers
and uncles, lost and
slaughtered
sons
And lovers.

Poem 35

Fine Dining
24/4/2016

You: left me

All alone

When the family

Went out,

To celebrate-

To enjoy, fine dining at

The Michelin Star restaurant.

And

I waited...

Patiently,

For my own choice selection.

I guarded our home

Where I

Snuggled down on the newly covered (white) couch

My favourite seat

With my bloody fresh bone.

Time passed. And,

I dreamed

Of the menu

That you

Chewed and swallowed:

I could taste :the venison

The chicken liver parfait;

Sheep's curd-encased in wafers;

Savoury canapés;

Herb inspired tobacco shapes

And my paws scrambled

And I scratched

As I thought of

The board of local cheeses

And the finale of

A la carte caramel

SEARCHING FOR AN OASIS

And ginger pudding

The coffees;

A cleansing tea;

The petit fours;

Until

I awoke with a hunger

Dribbling at

The odour of cake

A real scent,

So

I sniffed and I

Padded around

Exploring, searching for it.

I sourced the waft

And lifted a blanket, where

My own delicatessen

Had been (carefully) secreted.

A present

Just for me-

The birthday cake

Thoughtfully wrapped.

It was

Easily opened.

My jaws snapped

Cleanly through

The presentation box

Which was-

Quite beautiful

A supermarket,sealed,encasing.

Mmmmmmm.......

The white fondant icing

Beckoned me

To savour

SEARCHING FOR AN OASIS

A slice of the dessert-

A cake

Shaped like a petal

Left

For my own participation

In the

Festive birthday celebration

Thanks.

So,

I had a bite

Then

Another

But

I did, stop

To save you all

Well,over a quarter

And

A torn box,plus

The ribbon

And ,most especially

The fondant pink petal centre.

Then

When you all returned

I, too

Was aghast

Of course-

It was shocking

No candles had been blown out.

Not to worry though

We can all enjoy that

at the next

Birthday, celebration.

Poem number 36

Microaggressions
12/11/2019

You never talked about your frustration but

I know that Mama said

That you understood about institutional racism

And how it affected your own life

And Mama told me how you fought silently for us

Challenged her employer

When her so called colleagues referred to her in code

As "that black cat"

And you had to try to redress

The insult

Without making an undignified fuss

You were forever the diplomat

I know that you were angry

After that meeting

Because when you returned

You

Sat in your chair

Chain-smoking

Hard

Trying to find a space

To breathe freely

In your own backyard

Tried to encourage us to feel safe.

Concentrated on communicating to your children

The need to ignore any name-calling or insult about

The way that we looked

Or if anyone told us that England was not our home

You told us that we were born here

SEARCHING FOR AN OASIS

And that we had

Every right to be free and to enjoy

Where we lived-and we believed it

Taught us how to proudly chant back

'Sticks and stones'

Made us believe the poem

Made others recognize this

Because, in sending us to Sunday school

Or supervising cricket games on the rec.

Conducting watchers to join

You encouraged us not just to fit in but to

Lead the way and to excel

Taught us from an early age

As other children played

We were busy being tutored

Learning how to read and to play music

Helped us to be the ones who stepped up

Above the crowd

To be different for the right reasons

Ready to deal with the insults which you expected.

And we were cushioned

Protected by you

And we were schooled

Educated by you

And we were loved

Cherished

Protected by you

Who gave us his genes?

And much more.

Gave us a map

To navigate our futures

 For the life that you had chosen

SEARCHING FOR AN OASIS

In England

For all of us, as

our

home.

Poem Number 37

Childhood Hurt
27/8/2016

Collecting
sheets of memories
sorting
every page
Photographs of
tortured touches

Never

Should have

Existed

the author
tries to   rub it out
to ease the pain away

Writing is not
an   exercise
where, pity
is   sought

It is only   an

Honest attempt to

forgive and to   release
the facts

to   headline

The growth of pain

Where

Chapters of life
were   underlined
with
contained   stifled

Secreted, inward screams
of   hurt

Where
were the protectors?
Where, an adult champion?

A knight?

Who should have
timely risen?

Erupted with indignation
to save
Innocence;
to battle

Against   the corruption of
a child's right to

Simpler   pastimes.

Surely

Memories   cannot   be
erased?
But these must be at first
forgiven
so that
a beginning may be made

Towards that   destination

In learning   to

Forgive

      Ourselves
and allowing us to
learn to forgive
          offending   others.

Poem Number 38

New way to walk
1/1/2017

Thrusting propelled wings, eject us

Cargold in the hold

We are, collectively expelled
Expulsed from earth's fertile soil

We are birthed
exploding into illuminating blue light

Quickly wrapped in endless horizons, soothed by
immaculate walls of moist cotton sheets of clouds
Cleaned refreshed, prepared by angelic midwives,
for our timely arrival

In this dimension, birds do not fly, only-black
specks of speed zoom

A similar newborn, marked by embedded encrypted
letters targets on a course
Out there, yet very near so that we can identify it's
parentage

They too explore cotton bulbs, which pool between
the Pyrenees
and, wisping feathers, collect into fluffy mounds
Enticing play within footsteps of ascending
elevators
And, I do, walk on clouds

Poem Number 39
A slight breeze 29/9/2018

Fluttering leaves

Eyelid rapid clicks

Of photographic moments

Captured filed and secreted

Closeted in sections

Stored and treasured

Pocketed in

Selective memories

Fluttering leaves spark

A momentary remembrance

Poem Number 40

Meditation
16/4/2017

No need to rush

I have won

The moment.

Time

To feel

See

Touch

Hear

Taste, the seconds of life

And, just be….

Birds sing

Just because.

The sun shines

When it wants.

Flowers bloom

When they can

Fruit ripens when

The time

Is right

For them

A breeze

Ripples

Along, my skin

Solely

Just for

Me

And, all flows

Seamlessly

In my world.

And,

I am content

To

Just, be…

Joined by a

Flying insect

A buzzing beacon

Of life

Together

We: congregate

In a thankful

Celebration of

Just being

And

Our lives pass

Irrespective

Of, our wishes

And, our wants.

Poem Number 41

Cleansing waters
13/7/2017

Peeling off

Pretence
taking
tentative steps
to smother
any   thought

Surround   a

Sinking   desperation
A goose bump clarity of
isolation
          where
teardrops   ceaselessly flow;

they merge

          With oils and soaps

Which are meant?

To cleanse

And

Sentiments are

Purged
otherwise
accessorised by
talented   acting

And covered daily in

Everyday   clothes

The temptation to
submerge
Immerse   who I am
seek comfort

In   another world   of
bubbling   release
requires, reaching

Reminiscent   memories
replaying, mindful
meditations   of

Laughter and

Contemplating

An escape   into

Happier roles
so that

I am not
enticed.

And
stronger hands
than mine
pull   me
back

Poem Number 42

An Inner Light
6/8/2017

Why?
Did I stop looking?

when,there was
So much more left
to discover

deep   dark clouds
may part, and show
a, small crystal blue triangle
of sky

Why?
Do we, shroud
light skies

That are
always there, only
masked, to us?

Shielding sheets

Are meant

To be cleared

Folded and put away

So that   uncovered

Gleaming, shining colours
meant for our enjoyment

May function, properly
and, cheer us

a drooping flower

Can   stand tall again
and reach

Towards the sunlight
enriched by   just
a single drop of rain
and, a single soul
may begin to quench a thirst
by learning to

Lift   their   head
look up
Stretch, with an increasing strength
Fly, towards the end of

Their, self-made

Rainbow

Poem Number 43

Wanting
15/9/2017

Empty
exhausting   hunger
Broken
ravaged   uneven   edginess
head and nerves are

Swollen   with ache
teeth on edge

Lack of

Productive   interactions
grasping   directionless

Out of reach

Sinking

Wandering   boundless

somewhere
the saviour, on call

Is   elsewhere

Dealing with
more important needs and matters

Poem number 44
Lightning
15/9/2017

Closed   darkness
indignant   singular
Fearless

black   to

A loss of vision
Slipping   backwards
letting go
floating
Escaping
one way track

On   my own
close
your eyes

And   wish

Your hurt self
Away

Poem Number 45

Overwhelmed
15/9/2017

Because
I am lost
Lost in You
Lost
without You

Poem Number 46

Trees of Life
2/2/2018

Withered roots from within
Snarled and crooked extensions
push to without
No blood of life
runs through these veins
only anger; hate; envy
emulates from the tight and twisted mouth

She wraps
a grasping branch
around my child
Presses a crusted and toughened exterior
withered from ages of sought confrontations
against the smooth cheek of innocent youth
And the furrowed surface of herself
begins to seep
the warmth and honesty
from my little one's skin

A smile breaks
crackling new avenues across her face
While my child trembles
and looks at me scared throughout the transfusion
hastily I unleash her
encircle my protective arms around my own
protecting her
from hate

Poem Number 47

Alive, Autumn
15/10/2017

We walked today.

And, the sand scrunched between my toes

With the warm sun, on my back

And, the rush of curling waves

Foaming against streaming seaweed paths.

We

Walked today

Where pomegranate trees swelled

And, juicy pink popped beads

Were gobbled by matronly birds

Confined, nestling hungry newborns.

We, disturbed them, when we passed.

And, almonds, unshelled lay

Encrusted and scattered around gnarled boughs.

Fallen from, feathered green bushes

And withered branches that

Had escaped watering from

The maze of man laid pipes and hoses.

We walked today

Amongst: sandy pebbled tracks, where

Rustic blueberry vines

Robbed of their harvest

Retained some berries.

Discarded in, heaped bunches.

Left, shrunken and rotting

Shriveled skeletons

Dangling from natural puppeteer strings.

We

Walked today,

And, sometimes

Your hand reached out

Squeezed my own.

No longer alone

But, in love, and

Singing a song, in my heart.

Alive and living with

The love in my life

And, your footsteps marching with mine

Poem Number 48

A NEW DAY
3/2/2018

When

Another voice

Demands to be heard.

To speak out for:

The oppressed and the dominated.

I stand.

So that

The voice of reason

Might be heard.

Above bullying and domineering dictatorship

I stand.

Forthright.

Head above the clouds of

Collective consensus.

And, shout

A heightened dissenter.

Rising above

The din of fear

Against which

We all should:

Stand.

And, be counted.

Do not tell me to

"Sit Down"

For: I shall laugh

Out loud

Because I choose to stand

But, I shall stand, because

I can.

Poem Number 49

Streets of Napoli
15/9/2017

Emphatic conversations

Staccato gestures.

I see: emotional interactions

Loving, lively embraces.

There are

Blaring, tooting horns

Couples, hand in hand

Adolescents, sharing secrets

Amid a backdrop of

Poster brilliant slogans

Which hang

Amongst, bright, religious relics.

There is a lack of spaces

Effusive culture, clashes in the

Stereo sounds of Napoli.

Sophisticated by dress and bearing

A lady, observes the

Mirage of cacophonies

From her balcony, overhead.

Open doors carelessly display

Ceilings of architectural brilliance.

On the streets

Mesmerising artistic antique backdrops fall

From graphitised monuments

SEARCHING FOR AN OASIS

Where cherubic netted

Grey statue still lives, sit

And watch, the

Hand to mouth existence.

Whilst, crowds

Celebrate and laugh

Suffused in

Conversational culture.

Cannabis bars sit

Alongside skeletal

Halloween crumbling figures who

Admire 'culture hotels'

Tattered and crumbling

Saturated by, heavenly smells

Of pastries and pizza.

Shop windows frame

Pristine cooks, procrastinating

Ministering to elegantly showered, seated,paying customers.

They are expectant but

Satisfied that, they can afford it.

Streets with shops with displayed titles of

'Bella Tit Salon'

Compete for attention, with children's laughter.

Ensconced within protective railings, which divide

Wardrobes, chairs and other furniture

Left on excremental pavements.

And, discarded squashed

Pizza pieces merge.

Poem Number 50

Lift my Soul
22/1/2018

Humming   constant
Ceaseless
          distractions
Sagging shoulders

Slump, in sadness

Unsettled inconsistencies

Need refreshing

Long for a
cleansing   calmer

Silence

Poem Number 51

The Apple Tree
14/4/2019

The apple tree begins to blossom
Blue sky frames the landscape scene
No artist could imagine
A finer picture
Photographing stolen moments
Capturing forever
The happiness of last night's dream

I saw

An audience of
loved ones
Who entered in the
Magic moments
As
Meditatively, I watched
Captivated by
A buzzing brightness
Of
Sensations
Bouncing from, the family gathering
Whilst spectators
watchers
Joined in   gladness
silently
Locked away the memories

I can hear the echo of last night's chatter in my mind
Feel the laughter

Shadows of a buzzing crowd
Engaged in expressive conversation

A ray of sunshine brightens
In my backyard
There is
Happy children's laughter,here
Sparkling eyes
Genuine greetings
Sharing chatter
Sharing platters of
Friendship
Connected glances
Happiness- shines and glows
In my backyard
Spirits soar
Lightly gaily dancing
Tripping over the
Whispering ghosts,who
Enter in the celebration
Sunshine shadows
On the wall
Making growing plants flutter
As they pass

Strutting sunshine,dancers
At the end of my backyard
Zig-zag crossing shadows
A solitary seagull soars
And captures
A new day
Of:' Possibilities'
Shining down
On my backyard

SEARCHING FOR AN OASIS

An
Early morning, freshness
Beckoning me from
Sleeping the day away.
Magical colors of dawn
Rise and strut with a new
freshness
clouds break, in my backyard
To a sunshine moment of calm

A
Pulsing gladness in my backyard
Shines upon us
Happiness in my backyard
Sunshine increases in momentum
Spreading, covering increasing expanses, growing
larger in my backyard
Happiness
Stretches further
Spreading into your backyard
And I know that
Happiness spreads

Assured that
There is
Nothing,nicer than to see
Growing,families at play
Fascinated by objects which
Adults take for granted
Innocence teaching us to
View assumptive patterns
See them in
                a, different Way

BIO

 Born in the Northwest of England, the daughter of Jamaican parents, Erica B Donaldson-Ellison is a child of the 1960's. A teacher as well as completing her nurse training, she managed care services throughout England and Northern Ireland for almost forty years. She published poems and stories in anthologies in the 1980's and 1990's From 2020 she is published on social media.

© 2021 Erica B. Donaldson-Ellison

Printed in Great Britain
by Amazon